VERY SIMPLE
RUSSIAN

ILLUSTRATED BY
KIRILL SOKOLOV

VERY SIMPLE
RUSSIAN

By
Irene Slatter

Simple Books Ltd
Sandgate, Folkestone, Kent

VERY SIMPLE RUSSIAN

Simple Books Ltd
Knoll House, 35 The Crescent, Sandgate, Folkestone.
Kent, England, CT20 3EE

First published 1991
© Simple Books Ltd

ISBN 0-904404-75-7

British Library Cataloguing in Publication Data

**A CIP catalogue record for this book
is availble from the British Library**

Distributed in the USA & Canada by:
THE TALMAN COMPANY, INC
150 Fifth Avenue
New York, NY 10011

Photoset in Souvenir Light 11 on 12pt
by Visual Typesetting, Harrow, Middlesex
Printed in England by BPCC Wheatons Ltd., Exeter

Contents

ACKNOWLEDGEMENT

I would like to thank Nadezhda Bushueva and Irina Sorokina both of the Maurice Thorez Foreign Languages Institute, Moscow, for reading through this manuscript and making many valuable improvements. I would also like to thank Elena Belova of Leningrad University for helping to check the stress marks throughout

IRENE SLATTER

1

Background to Russian

In the second half of the ninth century the Cyrillic alphabet was devised by two monks (brothers), St Cyril and St Methodius. Up to this time Greek was used as well as some form of early Russian. Originally the Slavs used Latin and Greek for writing and a monk by the name of Khrabr remarked in an undated comment 'Roman and Greek characters had to be used but this was inconvenient ... How can one write correctly in Greek characters, such Slavonic words as *bogh, zhivot, tserkov, chayanie* or *shirota?*' (These old

Russian words mean God, life, church, hope, breadth). There are many Slavonic sounds which do not correspond with sounds from the Greek and Latin alphabets and therefore St Cyril and St Methodius 'created 38 characters some of which resemble Greek letters, others being for Slavonic sounds.'

The brothers did not invent the language but just created a Slavonic alphabet and the conversion to Christianity affected the language of the Russian people and established the written language once and for all. The services of the church were conducted in Church Slavonic which was understood by everyone and not in Latin and Greek as in Western Europe. A written literature based on church teachings began to develop and soon covered other subjects. Some of the writing was written in Church Slavonic, some of it in Old Russian and others were in a mixture of both.

Over the centuries the language continued to develop. For example, it absorbed Tartar words and after Peter the Great (1682-1725) had opened up Russia to West European influences, French, German and English words were incorporated into Russian.

After the Russian Revolution of 1917 the Russian alphabet was simplified to the alphabet of 32 letters used today. And now that there is so much communication between countries words are commonly borrowed by different languages; metro, taxi and kafe, for example, have become Russian words while sputnik, cosmonaut and perestroika have become English words.

The Alphabet, Stress & Pronunciation

The Alphabet can be divided into three groups to make it easier to learn.

1. *Those letters that look like English and have English sounds:*

А а	—	a	—	buck
К к	—	k	—	kite
О о	—	o	—	cot
М м	—	m	—	mother

2. *Those letters which have English sounds, but look different:*

Б б	—	b	—	brother
В в	—	v	—	vest
Г г	—	g	—	gate

Д д	—	d	—	**d**oor
Е е	—	ye	—	**ye**t
Л л	—	l	—	**L**ondon
З з	—	z	—	sei**z**e
И и	—	ee	—	f**ee**t
Н н	—	n	—	**n**ormal
П п	—	p	—	**p**aper
Р р	—	r	—	**r**adio
С с	—	s	—	**s**tove
Т т	—	t	—	**t**on
У у	—	oo	—	c**oo**l
Ф ф	—	f	—	**f**ather
Ч ч	—	ch	—	crun**ch**
Ш ш	—	sh	—	**sh**abby

3. *Those letters which look different and have Russian sounds although some of these sounds can correspond to some English sounds:*

Ё ё	—	yo	—	**yo**ur
Ж ж	—	zh	—	mea**s**ure
Й й	—	is the y in the word toy		
Х х	—	kh	—	lo**ch**
Ц ц	—	ts/tz	—	fi**ts**
Щ щ	—	shch	—	fre**sh ch**eese
Ы ы	—	the nearest is the **i** in the word ill		
Э э	—	e	—	as in the word g**e**t
Ю ю	—	u	—	**u**niverse
Я я	—	ya	—	**ya**rd
Ъ ъ	—	hard sign	no sound	
Ь ь	—	soft sign	no sound	

STRESS AND PRONUNCIATION

Stress is very important in the Russian language and can affect how a word is pronounced. All words of more than one syllable have a part of them which is stressed more strongly. The stressed syllable and vowel is pronounced more clearly and more drawn out. The unstressed syllables and vowels are pronounced less distinctly. You will notice when reading this book that in some Russian words, when **o** is the vowel in the first syllable it is pronounced like an **a** and I have transliterated the letters as they are spoken, not as they are written, for example:

вокзал written with an **o** but pronounced *vagzál* — station.

This also occurs when the o is unstressed at the middle or end of a word. The vowels **e** and **я** are also affected by stress — when they appear in a word before a stressed syllable they are pronounced in a less distinct way and sound more like the Russian **и** — i for example:

сестра — is pronounced *sistrá* — sister.

There are also hard and soft consonants in Russian and sometimes these consonants are followed by a soft sign **ь** which you will see. I have explained all this briefly not to worry you but to try and explain why I have transliterated words the way I have. I have also transliterated the **ть** and **ц** by using the English *tz* — this is for the convenience of the reader, although in a strict linguistic sense there should be a difference. But they sound similar.

3

Arriving in Russia

IMMIGRATION AND CUSTOMS

There are various points of entry when travelling to the Soviet Union. If you are flying then you will arrive in Moscow or Leningrad. If you are going by train you will enter the Soviet Union at Brest on the Polish/Russian frontier and if you are going by ship you will arrive either in Leningrad or one of the Black Sea ports. In all cases the formalities are the same although the procedures vary according to where you are. For example, if you are travelling to Russia by train across Europe the customs or immigration officials come onto the train. This is also true when travelling by ship. Do not be alarmed if the train stays a long time and is shunted about at Brest. This is because the train rails are wider in Russia than in the rest of Europe and therefore the gauge has to be made to fit.

The border guard will ask you:

> Vash *páspart i víza, pazhálusta* — your passport and visa please.

You could answer:

> *Vot, pazhálusta* — here it is.

If you are on a boat or train the customs officials will come to you. However if you arrive, for example, at Moscow airport you will have to go through customs. There are no porters but there are trolleys and you will need a rouble to use them. If business people travel regularly to the Soviet Union they will be aware of this and have a rouble put aside but otherwise not having a rouble means that you will have to carry your cases yourself.

There are now two channels for customs: one — something to declare and the other nothing to declare. However, the 'Nothing to Declare' channel is frequently not in use and arrivals are therefore checked through individually:

> *Vot mayá deklarátsiya móy bagázh iz (tryókh) myest*
> Here is my declaration and I have (three) pieces of luggage.
> *éta maí líchniye vyéshchi* — these are my personal things

When you fill in your customs declaration form you will see that they ask you how much money you are bringing into the Soviet Union. It is important to list everything i.e. travellers cheques, your own currency and cheque cards like Access/Visa. You will also see that you are not allowed to bring in fresh meat, seeds, guns and drugs. The customs official could ask to see your money:

> *Skól'ka valyúti u vas?* How much currency do you have?
> *Pakazhítye, pazhálusta?* — Can I see it please?

Your answer would be when you show your money:

> *Vot, pazhálusta* — Here it is.

Once the customs officer is satisfied he/she will say:

> *Dosmótr akónchen, spasíbo — Da svidániya* The inspection is over thank you — Goodbye.

You could reply:

> *Spasíba, da svidániya* — thank you and goodbye.

Like people everywhere the Russians are delighted if you try to speak to them in their own language. Many people now travel to the Soviet Union for a variety of reasons and they are quite used to foreigners who are no longer the object of curiosity they used to be. You will probably meet many different nationalities in Russia but they will all be able to speak some Russian as it is the first foreign language taught in the schools of all the republics.

If you are travelling as a member of a tourist group you will be met at the airport by your interpreter and guide and taken by bus probably to your hotel. Similarly, if you are a businessman you will also be met. If you are on your own arrangements will have been made to take you to wherever you are going. There are no stations

15

near the airports. Leningrad airport is serviced by local buses and taxis as is Moscow airport.

If you are travelling to another town from either of these airports you will have to go into the city to pick up your connection. If you are flying you will simply have to change planes. In Leningrad the same airport is used for internal and external flights, whereas in Moscow there are two different terminals, some distance from each other.

There are only a few shops in the airport itself, so do not plan to buy anything much there except duty-free goods and Russian souvenirs.

USEFUL WORDS AND PHRASES

Vot — here is/here are
Pazhálusta — please
spasíba — thank you
da svidániya — goodbye
mózhna — is it possible/may I

GRAMMATICAL NOTE

You may have noticed the word *Vot* here is/here are — this is useful to show something and after it you just add the word you want to show e.g. *Vot páspart* — here is my passport.

SIGNS YOU WILL SEE:
Паспортный Контпоь – *páspartniy kontról* — passport control

Таможня — *tamózhnya* — customs

Сувениры — *suviníri* — souvenirs

Подарки — *padárki* — gifts

Буфет — *bufyét* — buffet

4

At the Hotel

Having gone through all the border formalities you will be taken to your hotel. There
are various categories of hotel in the Soviet
Union depending on how you travel and what
kind of arrangements have been made for you.
If you are travelling on business you will be
staying at one of the most luxurious hotels in
the centre of Moscow, like the Metropole, or
the National. These hotels will provide
everything you could need. Your rooms will be
very comfortable with telephone, television,
even a fridge and of course a private bathroom.
There are foreign currency bars and very often
these are frequented by Russian prostitutes who
want to earn valuable foreign currency and
charge minimum 100 dollars a time.

If you are travelling with a tourist group you will be in a comfortable hotel such as, for instance, the Russia which is very central in Moscow or you could be further out in, for example, the Ukraina Hotel. These hotels also have all conveniences in their rooms, telephones and private bathroom. However, if you are travelling in a student group your hotel could be very basic with 2/3 people in a room and without private bathrooms or toilets. They could be even on another floor.

When you arrive at your hotel you will be asked for your passport in order to register:

> *Razrishíte vash páspart* — may I have your passport
>
> *Vot móy páspart* — here is my passport
>
> *Kagdá ya magú paluchítz svóy páspart abrátna?* — when can I get my passport back?

After registering you will be given your room number:

> *vash nómir na ... etazhé* — Your room is on the ... floor

You will be given a card with the name of your hotel in Russian and your room number. It is important to keep this with you because without it the hotel doorman may not let you in. This regulation is imposed in order to try to prevent the prostitutes and foreign currency speculators from coming into the hotel.

You may find a desk in the corridor where your room is and there may be a person sitting there to give out the room keys. Such people used to have to report anything unusual happening but now in the more open atmosphere of glasnost they are being withdrawn.

You may want to ask for the following:

prinisítye myhné pazhálusta — please bring me
míla — soap
palatyéntse — a towel
tualétnuyu bumágu — toilet paper
yishchó adnó adiyála — another blanket
yishchó adnú padúshku — another pillow

or you may want some of your meals in your room:

prashú prinestí mnhyé v nómir — I would like to have in my room
záftrak — breakfast
abyét — dinner
úzhin — supper

If not you will have to ask the time of your meals:

f-katóram chisú — What time is ...
záftrak — breakfast
abyét — dinner
úzhin — supper

You may wish to be woken at a particular time:

razbudítye minyá pazhálusta v palavínu vas mova — wake me please at 7.30.

Once you are settled in your room you will have to find out where everything is in your hotel (see below).

At the Service Bureau you can ask various questions:

gdyé nakhóditsa balshói tiátr? — where is the Bolshoi theatre?
kinó — cinema
muzyéy — museum
galiryéya — gallery
gdyé mózhna kupítz suviníri? — where can I buy souvenirs?

gdyé mózhna pogláditz kastyúm? — where can I have my suit pressed?

kagdá atkriváetsa ristarán/bar? — when does the restaurant/bar open?

zakaz'hítye mnyé pazhálusta dva/tri bilyéta v tiátr/kinó — please book me two/three tickets for the theatre/cinema

vízavetye mnyé pazhálusta taksí — please get me a taxi.

You may need to use the telephone — here are several useful phrases:

zdyés primóye saidinyeniye íli chíris kamutátor? —can I dial directly or do I have to go through the operator?

dáyte pazhálusta tilifónnuyu knígu —give me a phone directory please.

mnyé núzhna puzvanítz v Lóndon/New York I must phone London/New York

primítye pazhálusta, zakás na tilifónniy razgavór — please book me a telephone call

skólka stóit razgavór? — how much is the call?

ya khachú gavarítz is svaivó nómira — I want to phone from my room

gavarít míster Smith — It is Mr Smith speaking

slúshayu vas — hello

vas prósyat k tilifónu — there is a phone call for you

vash nómer zányat — the phone is engaged

u vas neprávilni nómir — you have the wrong number

GRAMMATICAL NOTE

All nouns have genders, masculine, feminine and neuter.

MASCULINE NOUNS

end in a consonant like tilif**on** — Телефон — telephone.

  „   „   ai like *chái* — чай — tea

  „   „   soft sign like *slovár* — словарь — dictionary

FEMININE NOUNS

end in a like *kníga* — книга — book

  „   „   ya/iya like *zemlyá* — земля — earth/ground

  „   „   soft sign like *matz* — мать — mother

NEUTER NOUNS

end in o like *metró* — метро — underground

  „   „   e/ie like *kafé* — кафе — cafe

  „   „   mya like *vrémya* — время — time

SIGNS YOU WILL SEE:

Гостиница — *gastínitsa* — hotel

Бюро обслуживания — *byuró apslúzhivaniya* — service bureau

Справочный стол — *správachniy stol* — information desk

Почта — *póchta* — post office

Стол обмена валюты — *stol abmyéna valyúti* — money exchange

Ресторан — *ristorán* — restaurant

Буфет — *bufyét* — buffet

Бар — *bar* — bar

Парикмахерская — *parikmákhirskaya* — hairdresser

Банк — *bank* — bank

Сувениры — *suviníri* — souvenir

Телефон — *tilifón* — telephone

Туалет — *tualét* — toilet

Мужской — м — *mushskóy* — gentlemen

Женский — ж — *zhénskii* — ladies

5

Eating Out

If you are a member of a group visiting Russia then all your meals will be provided for you. If you are on a business trip, your hosts will have arranged for you to eat either in your hotel or in a restaurant. You may also wish to go on your own to a restaurant of your own choice.

In Russia there are three different types of eating places. A restaurant is more expensive and smarter than a cafe, which is more expensive in turn than a dining-room which is equivalent to a poor cafeteria and does not sell alcohol. Cafes and dining-rooms are just for eating. You may want to enjoy an evening out in a restaurant which can offer greater variety in food and drinks. There is music and dancing and smoking is allowed here although not in cafes and dining-rooms. Russians go to restaurants not only to have a meal out but also for a celebration.

When you go into a restaurant you will have to leave your coats in the cloakroom — *gardirob*. The cloakroom attendant will give you *namirok* — a ticket/tag with a number on it in order to collect the coats later.

You will then go and choose a table or be seated at one by the head waiter. You could say:

> *mnyé/nam núzhen stol na* — I/we would like a table for
> > *dvaíkh* — two
> > *traíkh* — three
> > *chitviríkh* four

If you want to choose a table for yourself do not sit down at one with a notice on it:

> заказано — *zakázano* — reserved
> стол заказан — *stol zakázan* — reserved

and if someone is sitting at a table you could ask them:

> *zdes svabódno?* — is this seat vacant?

The answer will most likely be:

> *da, kanéchno* — yes, of course   or
> *izvinítye, zdes zánjato* — it is reserved

In many of the very good restaurants and hotels the menu is written in four languages — Russian, English, French and German. To order, therefore, all you have to do is point out the items you want and say:

> *prinisítyete — pazhálusta?* — could I have this please?

The waiter could answer either: *kharashó* or again *pazhálusta* — yes, of course.

He could say:

> *étava u nas sivódnya nyét* — we don't have that today.

When you want to order wine, vodka, mineral water or coke you must say exactly how much you want as one vodka could be taken to mean one bottle of vodka. So the waiter could ask you:

skólka vódki? — how much vodka?

You would reply:

vódki-sto gram — 100 grams of vodka
odnú butílku viná/piva — a bottle of wine/ beer

When you have finished your meal you could ask the waiter for the bill:

shchot pazhálusta — the bill please

And if you enjoyed the meal you could add:

bíla óchin fkúsna — it was delicious
spasíba i da svidániya — thank you and goodbye

The Russians do not drink tap water. At meals the choice is usually mineral water, juice, beer or coke. A wide variety of fruit juices is available from street kiosks and shops. Russian ice-cream is also very good as can be food from the other republics; so, if you have the opportunity, go to an Armenian or Georgian restaurant.

GOOD RESTAURANTS IN MOSCOW

Арагви — Arágvi
Арарат — Ararát
Арбат — Arbát
Баку — Bakú
Метрополь — Metropóle
Москва — Moskvá
Националь — Nationál
Прага — Prága
Россия — Rossíya
Славянский Базар — Slavyánsky bazár
София — Sofía

Узбекистан — Usbekistán
Украина — Ukraína
Центральный — Tzentrálni

GOOD RESTAURANTS IN LENINGRAD

Астория — Astória
Европейская — Européiskaya
Ленинград — Leningrád
Кавказский — Kavkáskii
Москва — Moskvá
Нева — Nevá
Садко — Sadkó
Советский — Soviétskii

Typical menu (these dishes can be found in restaurants all over Russia):

ЗАКУСКИ   ZAKÚSKI — HORS D'OEUVRES

икра — *ikrá* — caviar
сёмга— *syómga* — smoked salmon
лососина — *lososína* — smoked salmon
осетрина — *osetrína* — sturgeon
осетрина заливная — *zalivnáya* — in aspic
осетрина с гарниром — *s garnírom* — with vegetables
осетрина под майонезом — *pod maionézom* — with mayonnaise
сельдь — *seld/seledka* — herring
кильки — *kílki* — anchovies
сардини — *sardíni* — sardines
ассорти рыбное — *assortí ribnoe* — assorted fish
ветчина с гарниром — *vetchiná s garnírom* — ham with vegetables
ассорти мясное — *assortí myasnóe* — assorted meat
салат из крабов — *salát is krábov* — crab salad
сыр — *sir* — cheese
язык с гарниром — *yasík s garnírom* — tongue with vegetables
грибы — *gribí* — mushrooms
салат из огурцов — *salát is ogurtsóv* — cucumber salad
салат из помидоров — *salát is pomidórov* — tomato salad
кислая капуста — *kíslaya kapústa* — sauerkraut

СУПЫ — SUPÍ — SOUPS

Russian soups are very good and very often are cooked with meat and vegetables which are eaten after the soup with a knife and fork. Soup is eaten with dark rye bread.

борщ — *bórshch* — [borshch —] meat and beetroot soup

щи — *shchi* — [shchi —] cabbage and meat soup (usually with dill pickles)

рассольник — *rasólnik* — [rasolnik] — vegetables and chicken ~~meat~~

бульон — *bulyón* — [buillon —] clear meat soup

уха — *uhá* — [uha] — fish soup

солянка — *salyánka* — [salyanka —] sturgeon soup/or meat soup

окрошка — *akróshka* — [akroshka —] cold summer soup

РЫБА — RÍBA — FISH

осетрина — *osetrina* — sturgeon

форель — *farél* — trout

камбала — *kámbala* — plaice

щука — *shchúka* — pike

карп — *karp* — carp

треска — *triská* — cod

ПТИЦА — PTÍTZA — POULTRY

гусь — *gus* — goose

индейка — *indéyka* — turkey

рябчик — *ryábchik* — grouse

утка — *útka* — duck

цыплёнок табака — *tsiplónok tabaká* — roast poussin with garlic sauces

котлеты по—киевски — *katléti po-kíevski* — chicken kiev

МЯСО — MYÁSO — MEAT

азу — *azú* — sliced stewed meat

баранина — *baránina* — mutton

телятина — *telyátina* — veal

шашлык — *shashlík* — kebab

поджарка — *padzhárka* — roast slice of meat

бефстроганов — *bifstróganov* — beef stroganoff

антрекот — *antrikót* — steak (medium)
лангет — *langét* — steak (small)
бифштекс — *bifshtéks* — beefsteak
ростбиф — *róstbif* — roast beef
свиная отбивная — *svináya atbivnáya* — pork chop
котлеты — *katléti* — cutlets
эскалоп — *eskalóp* — escalope
шницель — *stnítsil* — schnitzel
сосиски — *sasíski* — sausages (like frankfurters)
разные блюда — *ráznie blúda* — assorted dishes
блины — *bliní* — pancakes
пирожки — *pirashkí* — pies stuffed with minced meat/cabbage/eggs
сырники — *sírniki* — cheese cakes
макарони — *makaróni* — spaghetti/macaroni
лапша — *lapshá* — noodles
омлет – *amlét* — omelette
яичница — *yaíchnitsa* — fried eggs
сметана — *smetána* — sour cream
творог — *tvorák* — cottage cheese

СЛАДКИЕ БИЮДА— SLÁDKIE — DESSERTS

блинчики с вареньем— *blínchiki s varénym* — crepes with jam
пирожное— *pirózhnoe* — pastry
торт — *tort* — cake
яблоко в тесте — *yáblaka v téste* — apple baked in pastry
мороженое— *morózhenoe* — ice cream
компот — *kompót* — stewed fruit
кисель — *kisél* — fruit jelly
чай— *cháy* — tea
кофе — *kófe* — coffee

SIGNS YOU WILL SEE

ресторан — *ristorán* — restaurant
кафе— *kafé* — cafe
столовая — *stalóvaya* — dining room
буфет — *bufyét* — buffet
закусочная — *zakúsachnaya* — snacks
гардероб — *gardirób* — cloakroom
стол заказан — *stol zakázan* — reserved
заказано— *zakázana* — reserved

GRAMMATICAL NOTE

There is a useful phrase:
mnyé nrávitsa — I like ...

just add the noun that is necessary e.g.

mnyé nrávitsa Moskvá — I like Moscow
mnyé nrávitsa dom — I like your house
mnyé nrávitsa abyét — I like the dinner.

Shopping

Shopping in Russia is usually quite a complicated (and sometimes infuriating) process.
You may well want to purchase some of the
many traditional and attractive goods that are
made in Russia, for example handmade pottery
and figures, wooden boxes, spoons, vases etc.
from the famous village of Khokhloma and of
course the required nest of dolls — *matrioshki.*
These can all be found in souvenir shops.

Подарки — *padárki* — gifts
Сувениры — *suviníri* — souvenirs.

You might also be tempted to buy an old
samovar or a picture which could typically
be found in a second-hand shop

Комиссионный Магазин — *kamisiónii magazín* — second-hand shop.

If you intend buying an antique or old item first make sure that you are allowed to take it out of the country. Also, be sure to keep the receipt as customs might insist on seeing it.

You can also buy many of the above-mentioned goods in a foreign currency shop called Берёзка *berióska*.

Good jewellery made of amber, gold and silver can be found in all the big hotels and in some specialist shops. It is usually good value for money. At the time of writing the exchange rate in the specialist shops is 1 rouble to £1 whereas if you shop in the ordinary shops the rate will be 10 roubles to £1 — therefore you will get more for your money.

The large department stores are called универмаг — *univermág*. These have many departments including a food department with various ice-cream and fruit-juice stalls

Мороженое — *morózhenoe* — ice-cream
соки—воды — *sóki-vódi* — juice and mineral water
There is гум — Gum in Moscow and гостиный двор — Gostínii Dvor — in Leningrad.

The shop assistant will write out a bill (check) which you will have to take to the cash desk. After paying you will be given a receipt which you must take back to the shop assistant who will then hand you your goods. Make sure that you keep your receipt as you will need it to return or change your purchase. It also acts as a guarantee for goods like cameras and watches.

In Russia books and records are mostly very cheap and of good quality. Books on art, books in English on medicine, economics, technology and politics and translations of Russian fiction into English are well worth buying.

You might want to ask for example:

u vas yést knígi Talstóva, Dastaévskava, Púshkina, Chékhova, Górkova — na anglíyskam yaziké?
Do you have the books of Tolstoy, Dostoevsky, Pushkin, Chekhov, Gorky in English?

Very often the answer is '*nyét*' as books are sold out almost immediately but you could be lucky and get what you want. You are allowed to look at most books and you will be able to see the price of the book on the cover. You can then take what you want to the shop assistant who will either tell you or write down how much you have to pay at the cash desk — when you go back with the receipt your books will already be wrapped and waiting for you.

As regards records, a stereo long-playing record will cost about 30p at the rate of 10 roubles to the £1. Beside the counters or at special stands are the lists of records in stock. All records have their own numbers and once you have worked out the letters you can ask the assistant for your choice so you could ask:

mózhna paslúshatz nómir sto dvádtzatz? — can I listen to record number 120?

and if you decide to take it you can say:

kharashó ya vazmú — alright I'll take this.

The system of payment is again the same as in other shops.

Since most of your meals are provided you will not need to shop for food but you should try some of the Russian ice-cream which is delicious.

As well as ice-cream you can buy drinks such as beer and kvas on the street. Kvas is a Russian drink made from black bread; it is delicious and very thirst-quenching. These drinks are often sold from tankers in the street as well as from stalls.

> *píva/kvas — adnú krúshku pazhálusta*
> beer/kvas — one glass please

You will also find stands and slot machines which sell a kind of soda water with different syrups. Here you take a glass and wash it yourself at the water fountain located on the machine. When you put your coin in the machine dispenses a drink, or you can ask the salesperson at a stand:

> *pazhálusta gaziróvka s sirópam — odín stakán*
> soda water with syrup — one glass please

or if you do not need the syrup:

> *bis sirópa pazhálusta —* without syrup please.

Some of the mineral waters are highly recommended and even have medicinal qualities from natural springs in the Caucasus:

> *pazhálusta adnú butílku minerálnoy vodí —*
> one bottle of mineral water please.

USEFUL PHRASES

> *pakazhítye mnyé pazhálusta —* show me please
> *skólka stóit? —* how much is it?
> *mózhna paméritz? —* can I try it on?

mózhna shtónibut darózhe — I want something more expensive

mózhna shtó nibut dishévle — I want something cheaper

pakazhítye tó zhe no drugóva tsvéta — show me this in another colour

vot éta pazhálusta — that one please

vot eta — nyét — ryádom — da éta — this one — no — the one next to it — Yes that one

gdyé mnyé platítz? where can I pay?

platítye v kássu — pay at the cash desk

pakazhítye mnyé pazhálusta yantárnie búsi — show me please the amber beads

pakazhítye mnyé pazhálusta gdyé knígi pa iskústvu — show me please where the books are on Russian art

or *gdyé knígi na anglíyskom yazikyé?* — where are the books in English?

SIGNS YOU WILL SEE

подарки — *padárki* — gifts

сувениры — *suviníri* — souvenirs

Берёзка — *bcrióska* — foreign currency shop

касса — *kássa* — cash desk

часы — *chisí* — clocks/watches

кольца — *kóltsa* — rings

броши — *bróshi* — brooches

соки — *sóki* — juices

воды — *vódi* — mineral water

дом книги — *dom knígi* — bookshop

грампмастинки — *gramplastínki* — records

мелодия — *milódia* — record shop

мороженое — *morózhenoe* — ice-cream.

7

Out and About

The first thing to remember is that the traffic in Russia drives on the right. These days there are many streets that are one-way and most have special crossings for pedestrians which should be used as much as possible because of the increasing traffic dangers in the big cities. Failure to cross the street at a pedestrian crossing may also attract an on-the-spot fine by a policeman.

You will probably want to explore the cities of Russia by yourself, so the first question you will have to ask is:

> *skazhítye pazhálusta gdyé ...* — tell me please where is ...
> *ristarán* — restaurant
> *póchta* — post office
> *univermág* — departmental store
> *aptyéka* — chemist

You will have to explain that you are a foreigner and do not speak Russian:

> *Prastíti pazhálusta — ya iz Ánglii (Amériki) — ya ni gavarú parúski* — Sorry I am from England (America) I don't speak Russian.

This is to make sure that the person to whom you are speaking will answer you slowly:

> *idítye nazát/abrátna* — you must go back
> *idítye napráva* — you must go to the right
> *idítye naléva* — go to the left

Some useful expressions you may read:

> *ya ni magú naytí úlitsu* — I can't find the street
> *f kakóm napravlyénii mnyé núzhna ittí?* — in what direction must I go?
> *éta dalikó?* — is it far?
> *mózhna daytí tudá peshkóm?* — Can I go there on foot?
> *ya ni pónil* — I didn't understand
> *skazhítye pazhálusta eshchyó ras* — tell me again please
> *pazhálusta narisúytye put* — draw me the way please

The Russians on the whole are very helpful and may offer to take you where you want to go:

> *ya pravazhú vas* — I will take you

SIGNS YOU WILL SEE

идите — *idítye* — go
стойте — *stóitye* — stop
остановка автобуса — *astanófka aftóbúsa* — bus stop
остановка трамвая — *astanófka tramváya* — tram stop
остановка троллейбуса — *astanófka*

tralyébusa — trolley bus stop

переход — *pirikhót* — crossing

подземный переход— *podzémni pirikhót* — underground crossing

перехода нет — *pirikhoda nyét* — no crossing

метро — *mitró* — underground/metro

You will almost certainly want to experience the Russian underground (subway) systems which in Moscow and Leningrad are very beautiful. The underground stations have a big red M on top of them. A metro journey costs 5 kopecks, irrespective of the distance. At the entrance to the escalators there are automatic barriers which have slots in them for the 5 kopeck piece. There is a small screen at the barrier which is red and changes to green when you drop your coin in the slot. All stations have machines for change and you can put in a 20 kopeck or 15 kopeck piece into the machine and you will get 5-kopeck pieces in return. There are also booths where you can change higher denominations of money.

There are very clear plans in all stations of the routes and station interchanges. In each entrance hall of the main stations there is an automatic map. You look for the name of the station you want on the panel, press the button and then the best route is lit up for you on the screen. The driver always announces 'astarozhna dveri zakrivayutsa' — careful the doors are closing. The next station is always announced on the train loudspeaker system but such announcements are often hard to make out, therefore you can ask:

kakáya slyéduyushchaya stántsiya? — what is the next station?

Since the trains are usually very full you could find yourself standing in a tightly-packed carriage. You could be asked by someone behind you:

vi vikhóditye — are you getting out?

Simply answer: *Da* — yes; *Nyét* — no

The same rules apply when you are travelling by bus, trolley bus or tram. You must enter by the rear door, move down (if that is possible) and go out by the front door. Only the disabled, elderly and people with small children may enter this front door. All the buses, trolley buses and trams have numbers written clearly on top with their numbers corresponding to the stop signs on the street. The fares, again irrespective of the distance, are 5 kopecks for the bus, trolley bus and tram. Bus tickets are usually available in books of 10 tickets for 50 kopecks in kiosks, on stalls in the street, hotels and even from the driver. The fare is put into the *kassa* (coin box) and you tear off your ticket. If you are far away you can ask someone to get your ticket for you:

prokompastíruytye adín bilyét pazhálusta — please pass one fare

SOME USEFUL PHRASES

skólka astanóvak da? — how many stops to?
kakím aftóbusam (traléybusam, tramváyem) mózhna dayékhat da? — What bus (trolley bus, tram) must I take to?
état aftóbus idyót da? — does this bus go to?
skazhítye pazhálusta kagdá mnyé vikhadít — tell me please when I must get off
vam náda soyití na slyéduyushchyey astanófke — you must get off at the next stop
vi seli ni na tot aftóbus — you are on the wrong bus
sichás vásha ostanófka — this is your stop.

SIGNS YOU WILL SEE

остановка автобуса — *astanófka aftóbusa* — bus stop

остановка троллейбуса — *astanófka tralléybusa* — trolley bus stop

остановка трамвая — *astanófka tramváya* — tram stop

вход — *vkhot* — entrance

выход — *víkhod* — exit

GRAMMATICAL NOTE

You may have noticed that we have used the word *mózhna* — may I/is it possible. This is a useful word and after it use any infinitive eg. *mózhna itití* — can I go. Or *mózhna sestz* — can I sit down.

SOME USEFUL EXPRESSIONS

gdyé zdyélat pirisátky na...? — where do I change for ...?

état póist idyót da...? — does this train go to ...?

ya idú právilna na pirisátky — am I going right to change trains

ya idú právilna na víkhod v górad? — am I going right for the exit?

vásha astanófka slyéduyushchaya — your stop is next

SIGNS YOU WILL SEE

метро (M) — *mitró* — metro

разменные автоматы — *razmyénnie avtomáti* — coin change machines

идите — *idíti* — go

разменные кассы — *razmyénnie kassi* — money change booths

к поездам — *k poisdám* — to the trains

двери открываются автоматически — *dvéri atkriváyutsa avtomatícheski* — the doors open automatically

для пассажиров с детьми и инвалидов — *dlyá pasazhívov s dyetmí i invalídov* — for passengers with children and for the disabled

не курить — *ni kurítz* — no smoking

выход в город — *víkhod v górad* — exit

не прислоняться — *ne prisolnyátsa* — do not lean on the doors

If you need to take a taxi there are a number of useful phrases you should know:

gdye stayánka taksí? — where is the taxi stand?

vízavitye pazhálusta taksí — call a taxi please

taksí svabódna? — is the taxi free?

You might get the answer:

nyét, ya zányat — no I am engaged

mnyé náda — na vakzál — I must go to the station

v — aerapórt — I must go to the airport

v — gastínitsu — I must go to the hotel

pazhálusta v anglískaye (amirikánskaye) pasólstva — the British (American) Embassy please

If you are going to a specific address it is always safer to have the address written down on a piece of paper so you could show it to the driver or say:

atvizítye minyá pa — étamu ádrisu pazhá-lusta — take me to this address please

astanavítis zdyés pazhálusta — stop here please

padazhdítye minyá pazhálusta — wait for me please.

8

Theatre/Cinema

It is often extremely difficult to obtain theatre or cinema tickets because they are usually sold out well in advance. As a tourist, however, the Service Bureau in your hotel will endeavour to help you through their own sources and if you are travelling by other means your business colleagues or friends may know a way of getting tickets — for the Bolshoi Theatre for example.

You could try to buy tickets yourself:

> *odín bilyét/dva bilyéta na záftra* — one/two tickets for tomorrow

The Russians consider going to the theatre is a special occasion and dress up accordingly.

The theatre usually opens at 7 o'clock with concerts starting at 7.30. The time of the performance is always on your ticket but if you are late you may not be allowed into the auditorium but instead you will be asked to go to the gallery until the interval. There are three bells which signify the beginning of the performance; after the third bell you will not be allowed into the auditorium. This rule is written on your tickets, posters and programme:

Вход в зрительный зал после третьего
звонка воспрещён

Entrance to the auditorium after the third bell is not allowed.

When you go to the theatre you will have to leave your coat in the cloakroom and any other things you may have except for handbags. The cloakroom attendant may well ask you:

Vam núzhin binókl? — do you need binoculars?

Binoculars are worthwhile to take for two reasons — firstly, they are obviously helpful to see detail more clearly and secondly, after the performance you will not need to queue for your coat as you will have the right to go to the front of the queue with the binoculars in your hand! Of course they have to be paid for so you can ask:

Skólka stóit? — how much does it cost?

They can cost from 30-50 kopecks — 3-5 pence. If you do not want them just answer:

Nyét, spasíbo! — no thank you

Then you will have to find your seat — when you enter the auditorium you will show your ticket to the person on the door and, if you want, buy a programme. You can ask:

Gdyé mayó mésta? — where is my seat?

If you are not shown to your seat you can ask:

Pazhálusta pakazhítye gdye mayó mésta —
please show me where my seat is

You must keep your ticket until the end as you could be asked to show it. During the intervals people usually leave their seats and go for a walk around the halls and corridors where there are exhibitions and photographs or they go to the buffet for drinks, ice-cream or sandwiches.

People usually do not show their pleasure at a performance until there is a break, either the end of an act or scene. There can be great applause and shouts of *Brava!*/bravo! are heard. At the end of a performance members of the audience sometimes go down to the stage and offer flowers and applaud in rhythm together.

As regards the cinema, there are no continual showings and queues (line-ups) are usual. Each performance (CEAHC — *sians*) has a newsreel, then an interval, so if you are late you can go in. You are not allowed to take drinks or ice-cream with you. Sometimes cinema tickets can be bought in advance so you will need to be clear when you ask (see useful phrases) for your tickets either for today or tomorrow.

USEFUL WORDS AND PHRASES

skólka stóit pragráma pazhálusta? — how much is a programme please?
vash bilyét pazhálusta — your ticket please
odín bilyét/dva bilyéta desyátii ryát, na syém chisóf — one ticket/2 tickets for the 10th row at 7 o'clock
na sivódnya — for today
na záftra — for tomorrow
izviníte — excuse me/sorry

GRAMMATICAL NOTE

Nouns in Russian are divided into six cases: nominative, accusative, genitive, dative, instrumental and prepositional. The numbers demand a genitive case after them — the numbers 2,3,4 take the genitive singular and all the rest take the genitive plural. That is why it is:

tri chisá — 3 o'clock but *syém chisóf* — 7 o'clock.

SIGNS YOU WILL SEE

театральная касса —*tiatrálnaya kássa* — theatre booking office
партер — *partér* — orchestra stalls
амфитеатр — *amphitheátre* — back stalls
балкон — *balkón* — balcony
ложа — *lózha* — box
левая сторона — *lévaya staraná* — left side
правая сторона — *právaya staraná* — right side
середина — *siridína* — middle
буфет — *bufyét* — buffet
курительная комната — *kurítelnaya kómnata* — smoking room
туалет м/ж— *tualét m/zh* — toilet gentlemen/ladies
вход в зал— *vkhod v zal* — entrance to the auditorium
выход — *víkhod* — exit

9

Getting acquainted & Conversations

It is most important of course to know how to say hello and the one word that will do for all occasions is:

zdrávstvuyte — hello — polite/plural form
zdrávstvuy — hello — familiar form

This is the word that you would use when you meet someone for the first time during the day and if you stop to talk you would automatically shake hands. The Russians always shake hands when they meet friends and acquaintances. You might also hear:

dóbroe útra — good morning
dóbrii dyén — good day
dóbrii véchir — good morning

In Russia Mr, Mrs and Miss were abolished after the revolution of 1917 and very often the word comrade — *tovarishch* will be used. Also, all Russians have a Christian name, patronymic and then surname. When you do not know someone very well you would use their Christian name and patronymic (which is taken from the father's Christian name). So, for example, a man called Ivan has a father called Peter (Piótr) — he would be known as Ivan Petróvich. A woman with the Christian name Tatiána or Tanya whose father is called Peter (Piótr) would be called Tatiána Petróvna. Surnames are also divided into genders. A man's surname could be Ivanov and his wife would be Ivánova. Thus, when you meet someone you could be asked:

> *kak vas zavút?* — what is your name? (lit. how are you called)

Your answer would be:

> *minyá zavút ...* — I am called ...

Russian Christian names have their own diminutives which can have very different forms for expressing various emotions from love and affection to annoyance. Therefore Piótr becomes Pétya which shows affection and Pét'ka shows annoyance. Similarly, Tatiána can be Tánya, Tanyúshka (affectionate) and Tánka for annoyance. Unless you know people very well do not use these names as they convey a degree of intimacy.

You may be invited to a friend's flat. The flats are in large blocks sometimes with shops underneath. The entrance to the flats, therefore, is usually at the back of the block where there is a large yard. Children play and the old people sit and chat here. The numbers of the flats are written in black letters on the walls of the buildings. There are no attendants, sometimes there are entry phones but very often they are broken, but most blocks have lifts which you will need to operate yourself. Remember that the ground floor corresponds in Russian to the first floor-*pérvii etásh* — so the first floor in Britain corresponds to the Russian second floor — *vtoróy etásh*.

You will be treated with great hospitality and the table will be covered with food. There are sure to be many toasts so you will need to say:

> *za vásha zdaróvye* — your health/cheers

The Russians will always clink glasses before drinking. When you have eaten enough you can say:

> *bólshe ni magú spasíbo* — I am full thank you

and

> *bíla óchin vkúsna* — it was very tasty

Your friend's relatives will want to ask you many questions about yourself and your families and will expect to see pictures of your children if you have them.

> *vi zhináti?* — are you married? (if you are a man)
> *vi zámuzhem?* — are you married? (if you are a woman

You could then reply:

> da, *mayú zhinú zavút* — my wife is called
> da, *moyevó múzha zavút* — my husband is called (see useful phrases)

USEFUL PHRASES

> *kak vi pzohiváete?* — how are you?
> *óchin priyátna paznakómitsa* — I am pleased to meet you

paznakómtis — let me introduce

maladóy chilavék — young man (even if you are not that young)

dévushka — miss or girl

kak vkúsna — how delicious

vi sámi éta gatóvili? — did you cook this yourself?

u vas yést dyéti? do you have children?

u minyá adín ribyónak — I have one child

u minyá dvóe (tróye) dityéy — I have two (three) children

skólka lyét váshemu sínu? — how old is your son?

skólka lyét váshey dóchiri? — how old is your daughter?

yemú (yéy) tri góda — he (she) is three years old

   pyátz lyét — five years old

kak yevó zavút? — what is his name?

kak yeyó zavút? what is her name?

You would answer using the same phrase but without the *kak* e.g. *yevo zavut...* — he is called...

gdyé vi rabótaitye? — where do you work?

ya rabótayu — I work

na zavódye — in a factory

v institútye — in an institute

v bánke — in a bank

v sovméstnom predpriyátii — in a joint venture

ya vrách — I am doctor

ya studént(ka) I am a student (the -ka is a feminine ending)

ya advakát — I am a laywer

ya rabóchiy — I am a worker

ya uchítel — I am a teacher

GRAMMATICAL NOTE

You may have noticed in the word hello there are two forms — most European languages except English have two forms for 'you': the polite and familiar. The polite forms are used with everyone unless you know them very well, like good friends, members of your family and children. This exists in verbs as well as forms of address. *Vi* is the polite form and *ti* is the familiar form.

Money, Numbers and Days

The use of money in the Soviet Union is not complicated and is the same in all the republics. You can only use foreign currency in the special Berioska shops, everywhere else you will need to have changed your currency into roubles which can be done at a bank, hotel, airport etc. It is illegal to change money privately.

There are two rates of exchange. In banks etc. you will get 10 roubles for £1 (5 roubles for $1) but in Berioska shops it will be 1 rouble for £1.

The rouble-рубль — *rubl* has 100 kopecks копейка — *kapéyka*.

There are notes of the following denominations — 100, 50, 25, 10, 5, 3, 1 roubles.
Coins — 1 rouble, 50, 20, 15 and 10 kopecks.
The small coins are useful.

5 kopecks for the underground, bus and tram
3 kopecks for soda water with syrup
2 kopecks for the phone
1 kopeck for a box of matches

NUMBERS

1	adín	19	devyatnádtzatz
2	dva	20	dvádtzatz
3	tri	21	dvádtzatz adín
4	chitírye	30	trídtzatz
5	pyátz	40	sórak
6	shest	50	piddisyát
7	syém	60	shestdisyát
8	vósyem	70	syémdisyat
9	dévyatz	80	vósyemdisyat
10	désyatz	90	devinósta
11	adínadtzatz	100	sto
12	dvenádtzatz	200	dvésti
13	trinádtzatz	300	trísta
14	chitírnadtzatz	400	chitírista
15	pyatnádtzatz	500	pyatzsót
16	shestnádtzatz	600	shestsót
17	syemnádtzatz	1,000	tísicha
18	vasyemnádtzatz		

DAYS OF THE WEEK

Monday	—	panidélnik	— понедельник
Tuesday	—	ftórnik	— вторник
Wednesday	—	sridá	— среда
Thursday	—	chitvérk	— четверг
Friday	—	pyátnitza	— пятница
Saturday	—	subbóta	— суббота
Sunday	—	vaskrisénye	— воскресенье

11

Business Russian

When you go to meet someone from a Russian firm you will already have made your appointment so you could say to the person at the desk:

Zdrástvuytye minyá zavút John Smith
Nicholái Ivánovich Petróv azhidáet minyá
Hello my name is John Smith.
Nicholai Ivanovich Petrov is expecting me.

The person at the desk will probably say:

Kharashó ya pasvanyú dlyá vas — Alright I
will telephone for you.

The receptionist will either ask you to sit down to wait for the Russian to come down or will escort you to the right place and introduce you:

Nicholái Ivánovich vot John Smith iz ánglii (amériki)
Nicholai Ivanovich here is John Smith from England (America)

You will be taken into his office and, if there are other people there, introduced to them. There will be soft drinks like mineral water and fizzy fruit drinks and you may well be offered coffee:

Vi khotítye kófe? — Would you like some coffee?

If you would like a cup you could answer:

Ni atkazhús spasíbo — I don't mind thank you.

They will probably exchange a few pleasantries like

Kak vam nrávitza Moskvá? — How do you like Moscow?

You of course would say politely:

Mne óchin nrávitsa Moskvá — I like Moscow very much.

And then you will all get down to business. Do not forget to have your business card with you, printed in Russian and English, and hand these round.

USEFUL WORDS AND PHRASES

delováya beséda — business talks
soglashénie — agreement
zaklyuchénie kontrácta — signing a contract
priyóm — reception
vstrécha — meeting/appointment
pirivótchik — translator/interpreter (male)
pirivótchitza — translator/interpreter (female)

vneshtorgbánk — the USSR bank for foreign trade

gosbánk — USSR state bank

MVT — Ministry for Foreign Trade

Targóvaya Paláta — Chamber of Commerce and Industry

teknícheskii — technical

economícheskii — economic

kommércheskii — commercial

targóvii — trade (adjective)

kommércheskoe predlozhéniye — offer

a *tepér pristúpim k délu* — and now let's get down to business

téleks (faks) iz Ánglii — telex (fax) from England

téleks (faks) v Ángliyu — telex (fax) to England

kófe bes malaká — coffee without milk

kófe s malakóm — coffee with milk

tzená visókaya — the price is high

tzená nískaya — the price is low

tzená srédanyaya — the price is medium

mirovói rínok — world market

vnútrennii rínok — home market

preiskuránt — price list

grus — cargo

u *minyá atkritii list* — I have a customs clearance

ya imyéyu litsénziyu navvós (vívas) — I have an import (export) licence

mizhdunaródnaya yármarka — International fair

12

At the Post Office

There are two types of postboxes in Moscow and the major cities — red for mail within the city and blue for international mail and to other parts of the Soviet Union.

A postcard — *pachtóvaya atkrítka* — can cost anything from 4-15 kopecks depending on whether it has a stamp on. You will need at least a 50 kopeck stamp for sending to Western Europe and North America. However, if you do decide to write a letter you can buy envelopes at any post office or kiosk again with stamps on them and sometimes pictures. Letters need stamps for 55 kopecks to Western Europe and America.

*Konvért i márki dlyá Ánglii/Amériki pazhá-
lusta*

An envelope and stamp for England/
America please

or *márki pazhálusta za désyatz kapéik dlyá
Ánglii/Amériki shest shtuk.*

10 kopeck stamps please for England/
America — six please

GRAMMATICAL NOTE

Notice the plural of stamp — *marka* — is *márki*. Most nouns have a plural ending in *i* e.g. *kníga* — one book, *knigi* — books.

There is something very useful in most Russian post offices that does not exist in the West and that is that if you want they will wrap up a parcel for you. For example, if you have bought some books or records and they are too heavy to carry home, all you have to do is to take them to the post office and say:

*Zavernítye pazhálusta kníqi v Ángliyu/
Amériku*

Wrap up the books for England/America please.

Once the books have been wrapped up you will get the parcel back and the assistant will tell you:

naphishítye ádres ... vot zdes — write the address ... right here

You must also write your address on the parcel. The parcel will then be weighed, stamps put on and you will be told how much it is. The post office also has a separate telegram counter. International telephone calls can also be made from most post offices. You will see the telephone kiosks inside the post office. A three-minute phone call from Moscow to London is around 4 roubles, and from Moscow to New York around 8 roubles.

To make an international phone call you must ring the international trunk office (tel. 271-91-03) but you can of course ring from your hotel where the switchboard operator will connect you which is much easier.

SIGNS YOU WILL SEE

почта — *póchta* — post office
телеграф — *tiligráph* — telegram
телефон — *tilifón* — telephone
приём и выдача корреспонденции — *priyóm i vídacha korrespondéntzii* — letters
приём и выдача посылок — *priyóm i vídacha posílok* — parcels
продажа конвертов, марок, открыток
— *pradázha kanvértov, márak, atkritak* — envelopes, stamps, postcards for sale.

Medical Matters

If you are taken ill during your visit to Russia there is no need to worry — a free medical service would be available to you because of the reciprocal medicare agreement between the industrialised world and the Soviet Union. For ordinary medicines you simply go to the local chemist. For example, you could ask:

> *dáyte mnyé shtó-nibut at rastróystva zhilútka*
> give me something for diarrhoea

The chemist could say to you:

> *prinimáitye tablétki dva ráza v dyén* — take the tablets twice a day

Many medicines are available for colds and other minor complaints and there is also a wide selection of homoeopathic medicines on sale in chemist shops.

S hould you need to see a doctor you could go to the nearest polyclinic. There are no general practitioners in the Soviet Union as such; instead you will see a doctor who just diagnoses your complaint and will then send you to see the relevant specialist — all of whom work in the polyclinic. So you must ask:

> *gdyé paliklínika dlyá inastrántsev?* — where is the polyclinic for foreigners?

A doctor, many of whom are women, will see you and ask:

> *shto s vámi?* — what is the matter with you?

You can answer with one of the relevant phrases.

If you do not feel well enough to go to the polyclinic you can ask to have a doctor come to you:

> *pazhálusta vízavitye vrachá/skóruyu pomashch* — please call a doctor/ ambulance

I f necessary you will be taken to hospital, but of course as hospitals everywhere are best avoided this is a last extreme, and if it is possible you will be treated in your room. Some Soviet doctors have become world famous like the eye specialist Federov. If you know that you need specialist treatment — for example you are a diabetic and need insulin injections — make sure you take your own syringes and needles as they can still be in short supply.

USEFUL WORDS AND PHRASES

> *V gastínitse yést aptyéka?* — Is there a chemist in the hotel?
> *mnyé núzhna likárstva pa étamu ritséptu* — I need this prescription made up

mózhna-li kupítz éta lilkárstva byéz retsépta?
— can I buy this medicine without a
  prescription?

dáytye mnyé shtó-nibut at — give me
  something for

    galavnóy bóli — a headache
    zubnóy bóli — toothache
    prastúdi — a cold
u minyá ... — I have a ...
    kashil — cough
    násmark — cold in the head
    naríf — abscess
    zapór — constipation
    panós — diarrhoea
    tashnatá — nausea
and *u minyá balít* — I have a
    galavá — a headache
    górla — sore throat
    paisnítsa — backache
    zhivót — stomach ache

SIGNS YOU WILL SEE

аптека — *aptéka* — chemist
больница — *balnítza* — hospital
медпункт — *myedpúnkt* — first aid post
оптика — *óptika* — optician
поликлиника — *policlínika* — polyclinic
    рентгеновский кабинет — *rentgénovskii
kabinyét* — x-ray room
скорая помощь — *skóraya pómoshch* — first
aid/ambulance

Going by Train/Car in Russia

Travelling by train in Russia is very comfortable and often more interesting than flying. It is easier to ask your hotel or business acquaintances to book your train ticket than doing it yourself. All trains have numbers so when you look at the timetable (see below) you can check your information.

Here is a typical railway timetable:

Расписание поездов «Москва–Ленинград»				
Timetable: 'Moscow-Leningrad' Trains				
Из Москвы From Moscow	поезда Train No.	Время отправления Time of departure	Цена Price	Прибытие в Ленинград Arrival in Leningrad

There are five types of compartment on Soviet trains.

1. *Óbshchii vagón* — is now found mainly in commuter trains (large open coach with many seats)
2. *Kupírovanii/kupéynii vagón* — four-berth compartments (most popular as they are the cheapest)
3. *Myákhkii vagón* — two/four-berth compartments which have softer beds but are more expensive
4. *CB-SV-spálnii vagón* — two-berths (sometimes beds)
5. *Vagón prayamóvo soobshchéniya* or *mezhdunaródnii vagón* — which are very comfortable, even luxurious, one or two-berth compartments. Some even have separate toilets. They are usually available on the long-distance routes and go across Europe.

The mainline stations have the Russian word *vagzál* (which comes from the London Vauxhall). The word *stántsiya* is used mainly for underground stations and smaller railway stations.

When you arrive at the station you will have to look for the train number. You may well see this sign:

поезд —	train 26
отправление 18.52 —	departure 18.52
платформа 4 —	platform 4

You may well need to hire a porter — their uniform is dark blue and they wear peaked caps. You will have to pay 30 kopecks per piece of luggage but this is worthwhile as the platforms are very long, so you could say to him:

Nasílshchik póist nómir tri, vagón nómir syém pazhálusta — Porter, train number 3, coach number 7 please.

Each coach on a Russian train has its own attendant who will take charge of your ticket when you board the train. If you want to keep it when you leave then you can just ask for it back: on all Russian long-distance trains you will get a glass of tea. The attendant will ask you:

> *Vi búditye cháy pitz?* — Will you have some tea?

No-one ever says no to this as it is a Russian tradition to have tea in trains and the question is asked for the sake of form and you could answer:

> *Kanéshna, dva stakána pazhálusta* — Of course, two glasses please

You are expected to pay for the tea and sugar when you get off the train but it is only 4 kopecks and the tea is very pleasant.

It is customary in train compartments for the sexes to be mixed. However, if you feel you would rather travel in a single-sex compartment you can always ask the attendant if it is possible he or she will arrange it for you. Smoking is allowed in the compartment. Be careful, too, of getting out of the train when it stops. This is because the stops are very short and you may miss the loudspeaker announcement. More than one irate foreigner has been left on the platform while the luggage, passport, money and friends go comfortably into the night.

As one might suspect because of the enormous distances involved, travelling by road through Russia can be challenging to say the least. There are areas of Russia, unlike Western Europe, which are not very populated and where there are few petrol stations. You will need to make sure, therefore, that you always have enough petrol for the journey. It is possible to go camping providing you plan out your route in advance and know where you are going.

USEFUL WORDS AND PHRASES

Gdyé póist nómir tri v Maskvú? — where is the train number 3 to Moscow?

Platfórma pyátz — it is on platform 5

Vash bilyét pazhálusta — your ticket please

Gdyé vagón ristarán? where is the restaurant car?

Chéres tri vagona — after three coaches

Pazhálusta razbuditye minyá v shest chisóf — please wake me at six o'clock

Mózhna pastilitz? — can I make up your bed?

Skólka kilamyétraf da blizháyshiva górada? — how far is it to the nearest town?

Pakazhítye pazhálusta na kárte dorógu — please show me the road on the map

Napólnitye, pazhálusta, bák — please fill the tank

Skólka lítraf? — how many litres?

Mnyé núzhna másla — I need some oil

Skólka másla? — how much oil?

Vodi v radiátor pazhálusta — please fill the radiator

Gdyé blizháyshi kémping? — where is the nearest camp site?

Gdyé mózhna astanavítsa na noch? — where can we stop for the night?

SIGNS YOU WILL SEE

Касса — *kássa* — booking office

Зал продажи билетов — *zal prodázhi bilyétov* — booking office

Вход — *vkhód* — entrance

Выход — *víkhod* — exit

Быход в город — *víkhod v górad* — exit to the town

Выход к пригородным поездам — *víkhod k prígarodnim paezdám* — exit to suburban trains

К поездам дальнего следования — *k paezdám dalnyeva slédavaniya* — to long distance trains

На Москву— *na Maskvú* — to Moscow

На Ленинград— *na Leningrád* — to Leningrad

Платформа — *platfórma No.1* — platform 1

Путь 2 — *putz 2* — line no. 2

Отправление — *atpravléniye* — departure

Прибытие – *pribítiye* — arrival

Расписание — *raspisániye* — timetable

В город— *v górad* — to the city

К такси — *k taksi* — taxis

К Метро— *k metró* — to the underground

Комната матери и ребенка — *kómnata máteri — i reebyónka* — room for mothers and children (women and children can rest and even get medical attention)

Зал ожидания— *zal azhidániya* — waiting room

Буфет — *bufyét* — refreshment room

Азс — *Azecs* — filling station

Кемпинг — *kémping* — camping

Бензозаправочная колонка — *benzozaprá-vochnaya kalónka* — petrol pump

Бензозаправочная станция — *benzozaprávochnaya stantziya* — petrol station

Авторемонтная мастерская — *avtoremóntnaya masterskáya* — car repair garage

Автосервис — *autosérvice* — autoservice

Вода — *vadá* — water

Бензин — *benzín* — petrol: A—72, A—76, A—93. The petrol is divided into grades with A—72 being a special type of petrol used in Russia